BURNOUT *to* BREAKTHROUGH

R.E.S.E.T.

When the Strong One Breaks

K. L. Davenport, M.T.S.

Pastor | Coach | Engagement Strategist

Published in the United States of America

ISBN: 979-8-234-04500-3 *(Paperback)*

First Edition

To every person who has been told their pain is not spiritual enough, their exhaustion is a lack of faith, or that being strong means never breaking.

This book is for you. Your reset begins here.

Contents

Preface v

The Pre-Work viii

Introduction 1

Part One The Breaking 5

Chapter 1 The Theology of Suppression 6
Chapter 2 The Weight of Scars 16
Chapter 3 When Church Becomes the Wound 26

Part Two The Framework 33

Chapter 4 Before You Release It 34
Chapter 5 R: Release 43
Chapter 6 E: Embrace 51
Chapter 7 S: Surrender 58
Chapter 8 E: Engage 65
Chapter 9 T: Transform 72

Part Three The Reset Life 79

Chapter 10 The Reset Life 80
Chapter 11 Resetting Together 87

Epilogue A Letter to the Future You 94

Appendix A: The Reset Workbook 96

30-Day Reset Journal 98

Appendix B: For Ministry Leaders and Ministry Workers .. 112

Appendix C: Reset for Organizations 114

About the Author 116

PREFACE

I know what it's like to run on empty for so long that being depleted became my new normal. I've had to battle with the grief of watching those I love close their eyes to time and open their eyes to eternity. I know what it's like to live in seasons where it seems my life is falling completely apart.

I want you to know something: before you read a single chapter, God was already in this moment. Before you opened this book or felt the weight of what you've been carrying. God was already here, working and preparing the path that would lead us on this journey together.

I wrote this book because I am a person who has survived burnout, religious wounding, grief, and the particular exhaustion of being the strong one for far too long. I wrote it because I spent years watching people just like you try to outperform their pain.

I wrote it because I believe the church has done a disservice to burned-out believers by offering Bible verses when they needed help, accountability when they needed compassion, and a to-do list when they needed permission to simply pause and rest.

I wrote it because I believe, deeply and without reservation, that God designed you for more than this. More than the exhaustion. More than the performance. More than the quiet survival you've been calling faithfulness. He designed you for a life of alignment, purpose, and genuine freedom. And it is not too late to get there.

Why This Book Is Different

There is no shortage of books about stress management, work-life balance, and Christian self-care. But this is not that kind of book.

This book starts where most burnout resources are afraid to go: with God. Not a sanitized, performance-based, smile-on-Sunday version of God. The real God. The One who met Elijah under a broom tree when the prophet wanted to die. The One who let the disciples sit in the confusion of Saturday before Resurrection Sunday arrived. The One who kept His scars after the resurrection. Because healing does not require you to pretend the wound never happened.

Burnout is not a sign that you failed.
It is a sign that you have been faithful
without being restored.

This book also goes deep into your emotions, your childhood wounds, your trauma responses, and the limiting beliefs wired into your faith without your permission. You cannot address the spiritual without the psychological. You cannot experience lasting healing by ignoring the whole person.

How to Use This Book

Read it slowly. This is not a book to speed through on an airplane. It's a book to sit with. To pray over. To argue with and return to. Some chapters will feel like relief. Others will feel like a mirror you've been avoiding for years. Both reactions are right.

Use the RESET Sessions. They are not extra bonus content. They are part of the work. The reading informs you. The sessions will help transform you. There is a meaningful difference between the two, and you deserve transformation, not just information.

Your reset is not a retreat from your calling.
It's the groundwork for it.

Individuals who recover the most from burnout are not the ones who gather the most information. They are the ones who slow down long enough to be honest, ask the right questions, sit with those answers, and allow their individual truth to reach the places they've been protecting. These sessions are designed to provide you with that experience.

THE PRE-WORK

Before you begin Chapter 1, take time with each of the three sessions below. These are not warm-up exercises. They are the foundation upon which everything else in this book will be built.

RESET SESSION

Reset Session 1: What Brought You Here?

Take time with each question below. Write honestly. Your first answer is usually the most truthful.

Before we go further, take a few moments to reflect on what you believe is the root of the emptiness you're currently experiencing. Resist the urge to give a spiritual answer. Speak your true feelings.

Reset Question: In what ways have my feelings impacted my health, my career, my family, and my faith?

Write it down and date it. Twelve months from now, when you look back, you'll recognize this date as the moment your RESET began.

RESET SESSION

Reset Session 2: Naming the Weight You Are Carrying

Take time with each question below. Write honestly. Your first answer is usually the most truthful.

One of the most clarifying exercises in my sessions is what I call the Weight Inventory. Most people carry a vague, heavy sense that something is wrong, but have never actually named what that something is. Burnout stays powerful as long as it stays unnamed. Naming it begins to break its hold.

Complete each sentence without editing yourself. Your first instinct is usually your most honest one.

The role in my life that currently drains me the most is:

The emotion I've been pushing down because I am afraid of what it might do is:

The person or expectation I am still secretly trying to prove something to is:

The thing I keep doing, even though I know it is crushing me is:

The one thing I most need permission to let go of is:

RESET SESSION

Reset Session 3: Your Reset Prayer

Take time with each question below. Write honestly. Your first answer is usually the most truthful.

Before you go further, take time to write a prayer. Not a polished, Sunday-morning prayer. An honest one. Tell God what you're actually carrying. What you're afraid of. What you're tired of. What you're hoping for.

____

____

____

____

My honest prayer to God right now is:

____

____

____

Before I Begin:

☐ I have named what brought me to this book.

☐ I have completed the Weight Inventory honestly.

☐ I have written an honest prayer to God about where I truly am.

☐ I am choosing to engage this process fully, not just intellectually.

INTRODUCTION

There was a moment when I realized I had nothing left to give. I was standing in front of a room full of people who needed me to be strong. The kind of strong I had always been—Dependable, steady, and capable.

But something inside me had quietly broken. Not loudly. Not all at once. It had been breaking for years, one neglected need at a time. One suppressed emotion at a time. One more thing I pushed through when every fiber of my being was begging me to stop.

It was April 2024. I sat alone in a hotel room in Washington, D.C., with thousands of people just steps away, yet I felt completely empty. The emotions I had silenced for years had finally caught up with me. I felt numb. Frustrated. Disconnected from the person I knew myself to be.

By every external measure, I was successful. I had achieved what many dream of. Promotions, recognition, and accomplishments that others admired and would have given anything for. But along the way, the very things I had once prayed for no longer fulfilled me. I was exhausted. In a complete daze. Wondering what had happened to me.

Of course, I kept functioning. The strong ones always do. I smiled. I spoke. I delivered. I showed up. But beneath the performance was a pain I could no longer outrun. A quiet ache. A soul stretched thin. A heart whispering it's time to stop and be still.

That moment was not my lowest point. The fact of the matter is, it turned out to be my turning point. It was the moment I stopped running from the truth I refused to hear. I finally sat still long enough to own it, experience it, and allow it to teach me what I needed to feel.

The strong one can inspire a room and still feel invisible on the inside.

The Burden of Being Strong

I pushed past the pain and finished what was expected. I did the job, met the deadlines, all while supporting and encouraging others. I was pouring from a cup that had been empty for a long time.

I knew for over two years that the path I was on was no longer working. I heard the internal warning signs, but I wrote them off as temporary noise. I could not remember the last time I asked myself what I needed. My life had become a checklist of roles and responsibilities, none of which brought me consistent joy.

The Loss of Self

In that moment, I finally accepted that I'd lost touch with the person God created. I was busy serving everyone else while neglecting my own needs. What I needed most was not another promotion or another goal. I needed something that aligned with my soul.

What Is a R.E.S.E.T.?

A R.E.S.E.T. is not just a moment. It is a movement. It is a sacred invitation to pause, to breathe, and to realign your life with the truth of who God created you to be. It is not about abandoning your responsibilities; it is about rediscovering your capacity.

> You do not need a dramatic breakdown to justify a reset. The quiet ache is enough. The numbness is enough. The sense that something has gone missing is enough.

R.E.S.E.T. is both a framework and a journey:

R — Release what no longer serves you

E — Embrace emotional awareness

S — Surrender the illusion of control

E — Engage what awakens your soul

T — Transform through intentional action

Each step is both spiritual and practical. Each one requires courage. And each one pulls you closer to emotional clarity, spiritual grounding, and the inner freedom that comes only from aligning fully with God's will for your life.

The Grace of Beginning Again

Life does not always unfold the way we imagined. There comes a point where we become tired of pretending to be okay. Being overwhelmed, overextended, and spiritually exhausted eventually takes its toll on our health, our families, our careers, and even our ministries and organizations. The good news is simple and powerful: God specializes in fresh starts and knows how to restore what life has attempted to strip away.

God never called you to be perfect. He invites you to lean into grace. Grace to grow. Grace to change. Grace to realign. Grace to begin again.

My Personal Invitation to You

I may not know every detail of what you've been carrying. Or how long you have held yourself together. But I do know this: there is more ahead of you than behind you. There is more for you to experience and to become. You do not have to live exhausted. You do not have to shrink your soul to fit your assignments.

Simply turn the page and listen for the whisper of reset that is there to keep you from falling apart. Do not wait another day to choose yourself. You have been hurting long enough.

Key Takeaways

- Burnout is not a character flaw; it is a signal that something is misaligned.
- R.E.S.E.T. is a spiritual and practical framework for reclaiming your God-given identity.
- You do not need another promotion. You need realignment.
- God specializes in fresh starts and never wastes your pain.
- This book is an invitation to return to who you really are.

PART ONE

THE BREAKING

Before something can be rebuilt, it must first be understood. These three chapters provide the language needed to name what caused the breaking. The theology that taught us to suppress, the wounds we still carry, and the church pain that distorted our view of God. This is not a place of condemnation, but a place of honest recognition. You cannot heal what you refuse to confront.

Chapter 1

The Theology of Suppression

How We Learned to Silence Our Souls

For most of my life, I had been taught that emotions were obstacles to overcome rather than information to be honored. In the church environments I grew up in, faith was presented as the opposite of feeling. If you had enough faith, you would not feel afraid. If you trusted God, you would not feel anxious. If you were spiritually mature, you would not feel angry.

This theology of emotional suppression created generations of Christians who smiled through suffering, spiritualized their pain, and praised their way through trauma without ever allowing themselves to grieve. I became a practitioner of spiritual bypassing without even knowing it had a name.

Feeling sad? Just count your blessings. Feeling overwhelmed? Just trust God more. Feeling hurt? Just forgive and move on. The problem with this approach is that it doesn't actually provide true healing. It just teaches you to hide your wounds while they fester beneath the surface.

Spiritual Bypassing: The Gospel That Skips the Pain

Spiritual bypassing masquerades as faith while numbing the very emotions that need to be brought before God. It uses spiritual language, practices, and beliefs to sidestep painful emotions, unresolved wounds, and the necessary psychological work required for mental, spiritual, and emotional well-being. Some statements may appear holy: "Just trust God." "God works all things for the good." "Count it all joy." But when used incorrectly, they can function as a numbing agent—a way to bypass the messy, uncomfortable work of actually feeling, grieving, and ultimately healing.

When someone shares their depression, they are told to pray more, and when a woman discloses abuse, she is counseled to forgive and submit. When an exhausted pastor is handed another Bible verse instead of permission to rest, that is spiritual bypassing. It takes the profound truths of Scripture and weaponizes them against human vulnerability, creating a culture where struggles are reframed as spiritual failures rather than opportunities for healing.

Spiritual bypassing doesn't make you more faithful. It makes you less free.

John 1 reminds us that God Himself took on human flesh. He experienced human emotion and felt human pain in the person of Jesus. Jesus wept. Jesus was angry. Jesus was overwhelmed with sorrow. If the fully divine, sinless Son of God experienced the full range of human emotion and suffering, how dare we suggest that faithful Christians should not?

A Framework for Embodied Faith

True spiritual maturity integrates faith and feeling, theology and therapy, Scripture and psychology. It recognizes that casting your cares on God (1 Peter 5:7) does not mean you will not also need to see a counselor who can help you understand the roots of that anxiety. It acknowledges that the joy of the Lord is indeed your strength (Nehemiah 8:10) while also recognizing that clinical depression may require medication and professional treatment.

The antidote to spiritual bypassing is embodied faith. A faith that honors the whole person and makes space for grief alongside hope. Hurting people need the ministry of presence. They need someone to say, "That sounds incredibly hard. I am so sorry you are going through this. What do you need?"

The Day I Learned Spiritual Bypassing Does Not Work

In June of 1996, my father died at forty-six years old. Five months—that's how long the form of cancer he had took to destroy him. I was twenty-one. Suddenly, I was the one planning an entire funeral.

My mother was drowning in grief. My younger brother was trying to process the incomprehensible. So I did what I had learned to do in our family, in our church, and from my upbringing: I suppressed everything I was feeling to handle the business at hand. I went to the funeral home and picked out the casket. I planned the order of service. I wrote his obituary. Reducing forty-six years of life into a few paragraphs that could not possibly tell my father's true impact and story. I did absolutely everything that needed to be done. Efficiently. Competently. While dying inside.

Then came the burial. I could not stand there and watch them lower him into the ground. I stood alone, about a hundred feet away from the family. And then the dam broke. Thirty minutes later, Farnell Jenkins—one of my childhood mentors—rang the doorbell. He saw my face and said quietly, "I saw how you pulled away at the cemetery. I wanted to sit with you and let you know I understand."

That is all he said. No Scripture verses. No platitudes. No spiritual language about trusting God's plan. No statements about God needing another angel. What I needed, what my soul was starving for, was someone who would sit with me in the darkness without trying to fix it.

People do not need spiritual bypassing. They need spiritual presence.

What Jesus Actually Modeled

Jesus didn't bypass his emotions. He wept at the tomb of Lazarus, even though he knew Lazarus was about to be raised from the dead. In Gethsemane, He said, "My soul is overwhelmed with sorrow to the point of death" (Matthew 26:38). He cried out from the cross, "My God, my God, why have you forsaken me?" (Matthew 27:46). Jesus was without sin. Yet Jesus was emotionally transparent.

The Psalms: God's Permission Slip for Honest Emotion

The book of Psalms is one of the most emotionally raw collections of literature in all of human history. David cries out in despair, expresses rage, laments injustice, questions God, celebrates, and mourns. Sometimes in the same chapter. Yet God called David a man after God's own heart. Not despite his emotional honesty, but perhaps partly because of it.

The Cost of Suppression

What we suppress does not disappear. It migrates. Emotional pain that is not processed eventually expresses itself through the body, through behavior, through broken relationships, through spiritual numbness. The person who never allows themselves to cry eventually cannot feel joy. The person who buries grief eventually cannot access hope.

Burnout is, in large part, the accumulated cost of suppression. It is what happens when you spend years loading weight onto a soul that was never permitted to set any of it down.

Beginning to Name It

Part of your reset begins here: with the simple, courageous act of naming what is true. Not the spiritual version. Not the version you tell others. The real version. The one that keeps you awake at 3 AM. The one your body carries as tension in your shoulders and heaviness in your chest.

You are not betraying God by being honest. You are coming closer to Him.

Key Takeaways

- ❖ Spiritual bypassing uses faith language to avoid emotional pain and leaves wounds untended.
- ❖ Jesus modeled emotional transparency. Feeling deeply is not a failure of faith.

You cannot heal what you refuse to feel. And you cannot release what you have never acknowledged.

- ❖ Embodied faith integrates theology and psychology as both are needed for true inner healing.
- ❖ What we suppress does not disappear. It migrates into our bodies, behavior, and relationships.
- ❖ Your reset begins with one courageous act: naming what is actually true.

Chapter 1 — Reflection & Exercises

When have you used spiritual language to avoid feeling something painful? What emotion were you bypassing?

___

___

___

___

What emotions have you been told, directly or indirectly, are not acceptable for a person of faith?

___

___

___

___

What would it look like to practice emotional honesty with God this week?

___

___

___

___

If Jesus wept, what is one thing you have permission to feel today that you've been suppressing?

____

____

____

____

Action Checkpoint

☐ I have identified at least one emotion I have been suppressing.

☐ I have written a short, honest prayer to God about what I am really carrying right now.

☐ I am willing to practice naming my emotions this week without judgment.

RESET SESSION

The Theology of Suppression

Take time with each question below. Write honestly. Your first answer is usually the most truthful.

Where in your life have you been using spiritual language to avoid emotional pain? Give a specific example.

What emotion have you been told (directly or indirectly) is not acceptable for a person of faith?

If Jesus wept, what is one thing you have permission to feel today that you've been suppressing?

Reflection Checkboxes — I am ready to:

☐ Stop performing spiritual strength and begin practicing emotional honesty.

☐ Name at least one emotion I have been suppressing this week.

☐ Permit myself to feel without shame or spiritual guilt.

☐ Seek a trusted person or counselor to process what I've been carrying alone.

Chapter 2

The Weight of Scars

When Resurrection Does Not Erase the Evidence

There is a wound in your story that you don't talk about at church. Maybe you have alluded to it in a prayer request. Softened it up a bit around the edges so it sounds more palatable and less devastating than it actually was. Maybe you have buried it so deep that you have almost convinced yourself it isn't there. But it is. And it's heavier than it needs to be because you have been carrying it in silence.

This chapter is about your scars. Not to reopen wounds, but to help you understand them. Because what you do with your wounds will determine the quality of your testimony, the depth of your compassion, and the freedom you carry into every room you enter.

The Theology of Scars: God Wastes Nothing

Before we look at Jesus' scars, we need to establish a foundational theological truth: God wastes nothing. Not your tears. Not your trauma. Not your burnout. Not your broken dreams. Not the years you feel were stolen. Not the innocence you lost. Not the trust that was betrayed. Not the exhaustion that nearly destroyed you. Nothing.

This is not toxic positivity. This is not spiritual bypassing. This is the bold, audacious claim of the gospel: that God is so powerful, so creative, so redemptive that He can take what was meant to destroy you and transform it into the very thing that equips you to help others.

> *And we know that in all things God works for the good of those who love him, who have been called according to his purpose.*
>
> **— Romans 8:28**

> *The God of all comfort, who comforts us in all our troubles, so that we can comfort those in any trouble with the comfort we ourselves receive from God.*
>
> **— 2 Corinthians 1:3–4**

Here is the redemptive economy of suffering: you do not suffer for nothing. You suffer to become someone who can sit with others in their suffering. The comfort you receive in your darkest valley becomes the comfort you offer when someone else is walking through theirs. Your healed scar becomes someone else's hope.

The Risen Christ and His Scars

After the crucifixion, after the nails, the spear, the mockery, the abandonment, the darkness, the death, the burial, and the silence of Saturday, Sunday morning came. Complete with an empty tomb and a risen Savior.

The resurrected Christ appears to the disciples in John 20. The room is locked. Not just physically, but emotionally. They are hiding, grieving what they believed was a failed revolution. Then suddenly, Jesus stands among them. Whole. Alive. Completely resurrected. His first words: "Peace be with you." Not rebuke. Not shame. Not disappointment. But peace. Then Jesus showed them His hands and His side. Jesus showed them His scars.

Resurrection Does Not Require Erasure

We often operate under a deeply flawed theology of healing. We believe that healing means erasure. If God heals me, the memory should disappear. If God restores me, the pain should vanish. But Jesus stands in the upper room as living proof that resurrection does not require erasure. He was fully healed and fully scarred. Completely whole and permanently marked.

The resurrected Christ, with all the power of heaven at His disposal, kept His scars. Because the scars were not evidence of defeat, they were evidence of victory.

Your scars do not mean you are unfinished. They do not mean you are broken beyond repair. They do not disqualify you from ministry, from leadership, from intimacy, or from purpose. Your scars reveal that you have, in fact, been resurrected.

The Scars as Credentials: Thomas and the Wounds

One week later, Jesus appears again. Thomas had said, "Unless I see the nail marks in his hands and put my finger where the nails were, and put my hand into his side, I will not believe" (John 20:25). Jesus, rather than condemning him for his doubt, met him exactly where he was: "Put your finger here; see my hands. Reach out your hand and put it into my side. Stop doubting and believe" (John 20:27). Jesus invited Thomas to touch the scars because the scars were the evidence.

The burnout you are ashamed of often makes you credible to others who are experiencing the same thing. The depression you don't talk about gives you authority to speak into someone else's darkness. Your scars are not disqualifications. They are credentials.

What if the thing you are most tempted to hide is the very thing that will authenticate your testimony?

The Difference Between Open Wounds and Healed Scars

There is a critical distinction between open wounds and healed scars: an open wound still bleeds. A scar tells a story. An open wound is active trauma. It is still raw, painful, and controlling you. A scar is healed trauma that's been integrated, processed, and no longer in charge.

If talking about something still retraumatizes you, and you cannot tell the story without falling apart. If thinking about it sends you into spirals of shame, hurt, and frustration, then it's still an open wound. It needs tending. In some instances, it needs professional therapy. It needs safe people who can support you and walk with you. Most importantly, it needs time. There is no shame in having open wounds. Jesus had compassion for bleeding people.

But if you can tell the story without being controlled by it. If you have processed the pain and integrated the lesson, then you no longer have an open wound but a visual scar. Scars say: I was wounded here, but I healed. I am still standing, and I can help you stand as well.

Stewarding Your Scars Well

Not everyone deserves access to your wounds, or, for that matter, to your scars. Some people will use your pain against you. You do not owe everyone your story. But someone needs your healed scar. Someone out there is sitting in the waiting room of the crisis you survived. They need to know that healing is possible.

✶ A Prayer ✶

God, You see every scar I carry. Both visible and invisible. You know the ones that people sympathize with, and the ones I hide in shame. I bring it all to You. Heal what still bleeds in me. Redeem what the enemy tried to use against me. Remind me that I am not defined by what happened to me. I am defined by who You say I am: beloved, redeemed, restored. Just like Jesus, may I bear my scars not with shame, but with the quiet confidence that says, "I went through it." God met me there. And I have overcome. In Jesus' name, Amen.

Key Takeaways

- ❖ The resurrected Christ kept His scars. Resurrection does not require erasure.
- ❖ Open wounds need tending; healed scars serve as testimony and credentials for ministry.
- ❖ Your scars are not disqualifications. They are evidence of survival and resurrection power.
- ❖ God wastes nothing. Not your tears, your trauma, your burnout, or your broken dreams.
- ❖ Someone needs the testimony that only your healed scar can provide.

Chapter 2 — Reflection & Exercises

Which scars in your life still feel like open wounds? Which have begun to feel like testimonies?

What would it look like to view your scars as evidence of survival rather than proof of damage?

What is one part of your story you have been ashamed to share? What has that silence cost you?

Jesus kept His scars after the resurrection. How do you feel about your healed wounds remaining visible?

____

____

____

____

Action Checkpoint

- ☐ I have identified at least one wound that is now a scar.
- ☐ I have named one person who might need to hear my testimony.
- ☐ I am willing to release the belief that healing requires complete erasure.

RESET SESSION

The Weight of Scars

Take time with each question below. Write honestly. Your first answer is usually the most truthful.

What is one wound in your story that you rarely talk about? You know, the one you carry in silence? Describe it briefly here.

Is this wound an open wound (still raw, still controlling you) or a healed scar (integrated, processable)? How do you know?

How has God already begun to redeem something painful in your life? What testimony is beginning to form from your scar?

Reflection Checkboxes — I am willing to:

☐ Acknowledge one wound I have been carrying in silence.

☐ Seek professional support (therapist, counselor, pastor) for wounds that are still open.

☐ Ask God to begin redeeming my scars for the benefit of someone else.

☐ Stop hiding the parts of my story that God wants to use as a testimony.

Chapter 3

When Church Becomes the Wound

Healing from Religious Trauma Without Losing Your Faith

This chapter is one of the most difficult, yet most necessary, in this entire book. If we are going to talk honestly about burnout in the Christian community, we have to talk about the places where faith communities have contributed to the very wounds they were meant to heal.

Church hurt is real. Religious trauma is real. And it is far more common than the church is willing to admit. If you have experienced spiritual abuse, manipulation by religious authority, public shaming disguised as accountability, conditional love framed as grace, or a culture where your worth was tied to your productivity for the Kingdom, you are not alone.

The Layered Nature of Church Hurt

What makes church hurt uniquely devastating is its layered nature. When a friend betrays you, it is painful. When a church betrays you, it simultaneously wounds your heart and distorts your theology. You don't just lose trust in a person. You lose trust in God, in spiritual authority, in community, in yourself.

Separating God from the Gatekeepers

One of the most important things your reset requires is separating who God is from the people who misrepresented Him. The church is made up of imperfect human beings. It was never meant to be the object of your faith. God is. Institutions and individuals fail. God doesn't.

Find a safe faith community. Not every church is toxic. Not every leader is unsafe. You may need time and discernment to find a healthy community, but one exists. Isolation is not protection but a wound that compounds over time.

Consider professional support. A licensed counselor or trauma-informed therapist can help you process religious trauma in ways that a pastor or spiritual mentor may not be equipped to provide, and both can coexist.

✶ A Prayer ✶

God, I bring You my church wounds. The ones I have been told I should not have, the ones I have been ashamed to name. I was hurt in Your house, by people who spoke in Your name. I need You to know: it still hurts. Help me see You clearly. Not through the lens of those who wounded me, but as You actually are. Heal what is bro ken in me. Rebuild my trust. Not in institutions, but in You. I refuse to let what happened to me destroy my faith. In Jesus' name, Amen.

Key Takeaways

- ❖ Church hurt is layered trauma. It simultaneously wounds the heart and distorts your theology.
- ❖ Jesus confronted religious abuse directly. He is on the side of the wounded.
- ❖ Trauma produces limiting beliefs that sound like spiritual truths but are actually defense mechanisms.
- ❖ You can leave a toxic church without leaving God. They are not the same.
- ❖ Healing requires separating God's character from the failures of those who misrepresented Him.

Chapter 3 — Reflection & Exercises

What specific church experiences created pain for you?

____

____

____

____

What beliefs about God, authority, or yourself formed during those experiences?

____

____

____

____

What have you unconsciously blamed God for that was actually done by people acting in His name?

____

____

____

____

In what ways did your church wound also distort how you see yourself?

____

____

____

____

Action Checkpoint

☐ I have named at least one limiting belief I formed from church hurt.

☐ I have distinguished that which is God's character from that which is derived from flawed human behavior.

☐ I am open to finding or being a part of a healthier faith community.

RESET SESSION

When Church Becomes the Wound

Take time with each question below. Write honestly. Your first answer is usually the most truthful.

Describe one specific way a religious community or leader caused you harm. What happened, and how did it affect your faith?

____

____

____

____

How has that experience shaped your image of God? In what ways has it made it harder to trust Him or His people?

____

____

____

____

What would it look like for you to separate Jesus from the people who hurt you in His name? What truth about Him do you need to reclaim?

____

____

____

____

Reflection Checkboxes — I am choosing to:

☐ Name the religious wound I have been carrying without permission to grieve.

☐ Stop confusing God with the people who misrepresented Him.

☐ Seek a safe community where I can be honest about my faith struggles.

☐ Give myself permission to be angry at what was done to me without feeling guilty about that anger.

PART TWO

THE FRAMEWORK

You have named what broke. Now it is time to build what's next. The R.E.S.E.T. framework is a spiritual and psychological roadmap. Five movements that together create the conditions for lasting transformation. Each step builds on the last. Take them in order. Take them seriously. Your whole life is waiting on the other side.

Chapter 4

Before You Release It

Why I Just Can't Let This Go

There is a moment right before release that feels like resistance. Not resistance in the spiritual sense, such as being rebellious or refusing God's will. But resistance in the physiological sense, where every cell in your body, every learned pattern in your nervous system, every survival mechanism you have developed over years or decades, is screaming at you not to let go.

Your mind says, I need to release this. Your body says, absolutely not. Caught between exhaustion and terror. Between knowing you cannot keep carrying this and believing you can't survive without it.

People do not hold on because they want to suffer. They hold on because something deep inside believes they have to.

The Four Survival Responses

Fight

Some of you learned to stay hyper-alert, scanning every room, reading every facial expression, anticipating every problem before it arrives. You became the planner, the manager, the one who cannot relax because relaxing feels like negligence.

Flight

Some of you learned to stay in motion. Always producing, always achieving, always doing one more thing so you would be valuable enough to keep. You became the high-achiever whose worth is tied to output because somewhere deep down, you believe that if you stop performing, you will be abandoned.

Freeze

Some of you learned to shut down. To disconnect from your feelings. To go numb, to operate on autopilot because feeling everything was too overwhelming. You became the stoic one who can function in crisis but cannot seem to access joy.

Fawn

Some of you learned to take care of others, prioritizing their needs over your own. Keeping the peace at any cost. You became the caretaker, the peacemaker, the one everyone calls in a crisis; however, you collapse into your own private pain as soon as you get alone.

Your Body Adapted to Survive

None of these responses is a character flaw. They are adaptations. Your body did what it had to do to keep you alive. You survived. But here is the tragic part: what once helped you survive may now be preventing your breakthrough.

The hyper-vigilance that protected you is now exhausting you. The performance that earned you acceptance is now burning you out. The emotional shutdown that kept you functional is now keeping you disconnected. The people-pleasing that kept you safe is now making you invisible to yourself.

You learned to survive.
Now it's time to learn to thrive.

Burnout: When Survival Mode Becomes Your Default

Burnout is what happens when survival mode never turns off. You were overextended, overexposed, over responsible. Somewhere along the way, your soul whispered: I am tired. Not tired like a good night's sleep can fix this. Tired like you are running on fumes, and the tank has been empty for years. This type of tiredness has a name: burnout. It doesn't happen because you are weak. It happens because you have been strong for too long without rest, without support, without permission to simply be human.

Elijah Under the Broom Tree

In 1 Kings 19, Elijah's burnout happens immediately after his greatest victory. He had just called down fire from heaven, defeated 450 prophets of Baal, and prayed for rain after over three years of drought—a mountaintop experience by any measure.

Notice what God does not say. God does not say, Pray harder. God does not say, Have more faith. Instead, God sends an angel with food and water. Allows him to sleep. Feeds him again. Lets him sleep again. Before God offered instruction, there was restoration.

> *Elijah was afraid and ran for his life. He came to a broom bush and prayed that he might die. "I have had enough, LORD," he said.*
>
> **— 1 Kings 19:3–4**

Before there was an assignment, there was replenishment.

Jesus in Gethsemane: Naming Before Surrendering

Before the cross, there was a garden. Before the sacrifice, there was sorrow. Before the surrender, the cost was honestly named. Jesus does not pretend. He names it. Only after Jesus acknowledges his true desire and feelings does he then say, "not as I will, but as you will." The pattern is clear: Jesus named His anguish before He surrendered it. You cannot release what you refuse to acknowledge. Naming comes before surrendering.

Release cannot happen in a body that feels unsafe. Your body has to feel safe before your soul can let go.

✶ A Prayer ✶

God, I confess I have been holding on tightly to what I should have released long ago. My body is tired. My soul is weary. Today, I choose to acknowledge what I have been carrying. I will not rush to surrender what I have not yet named. Meet me here, in my honest place. I trust that release is possible. Give me the courage to begin. In Jesus' name, Amen.

Key Takeaways

- Your body may resist release because it has been wired for survival, not surrender.
- Fight, flight, freeze, and fawn are not character flaws. They are adaptations to unsafe environments.
- Burnout occurs when survival mode becomes your permanent default setting.
- God's response to Elijah's burnout was rest and restoration before reassignment.
- You cannot release what you have not first acknowledged. Naming comes before surrendering.

Chapter 4 — Reflection & Exercises

Which survival response resonates most with you: fight, flight, freeze, or fawn? Give a recent example.

____

____

____

____

What do you believe would happen if you slowed down and stopped carrying everything you're currently holding?

____

____

____

____

Like Elijah under the broom tree, what does your soul need right now before you take another step forward?

____

____

____

____

Where in your life has your survival response become your primary operating system?

____

____

____

____

Action Checkpoint

- ☐ I have identified the primary survival pattern I default to under stress.
- ☐ I have given my body what it needs before I attempt to give anyone else more of me.
- ☐ I have named the fear that is keeping me from releasing what I know I need to let go.
- ☐ I have practiced one act of intentional rest or replenishment this week.

RESET SESSION

Understanding Your Resistance

Take time with each question below. Write honestly. Your first answer is usually the most truthful.

Which of the four stress responses — fight, flight, freeze, or fawn — feels most familiar to you? Describe a recent situation where you defaulted to this response.

What do you believe would happen if you slowed down and stopped carrying everything you are currently holding? What are you most afraid of?

Like Elijah under the broom tree, what does your soul need right now before you take another step forward? Be specific.

Reflection Checkboxes — This week, I will:

☐ Identify the primary survival pattern I default to under stress.

☐ Give my body what it needs before I attempt to give anyone else more of me.

☐ Name the fear that is keeping me from releasing what I know I need to let go.

☐ Practice one act of intentional rest or replenishment this week.

Chapter 5

R: Release

What No Longer Serves You

The Weight of What You're Carrying

Every person reading this is carrying something they were never meant to carry. You may have taken it on willingly, out of love, loyalty, or survival. You may have had it placed on you by someone else's expectations or dysfunction. But at some point, it stopped being a calling and became a crushing weight.

What Release Is Not

Release is not irresponsibility. It is not abandonment. It is not giving up. Release is the spiritual act of laying down what God never intended for you to carry. The people, situations, and things you've outgrown.

The Spiritual Call to Release

Scripture is full of invitations to release, surrender, and lay down what is too heavy. We are told to cast our cares on the Lord because He will sustain us, to throw off everything that hinders, and to come to Him when we are weary and burdened. These are not poetic suggestions. They are divine instructions for how to live free.

Three Essential Releases

Release the Pressure to Be Everything: You are not called to be superhuman. God didn't call you to save everyone. He called you to be faithful with what He assigned to you.

Release Roles That No Longer Fit: Sometimes God calls you to grow beyond the identity you built to survive. Walking away from these roles is often a necessary part of growth.

Release the Pain You Keep Replaying: Some memories have become sources of bondage you revisit over and over. It's important that you release the loop, the guilt, and the shame.

The Sacred Exchange

Every time you release something that no longer serves you, you create space for something new. Every surrender makes room for renewal. This is the sacred exchange: when you let go of what is breaking you, God fills you with what will build you.

The Art of Leaving Well

Many people find themselves trapped. Unable to leave relationships, jobs, ministries, or positions. Not because they lack the courage to go, but because they fear the fallout that follows. Let's be honest: everyone teaches you how to show up. Almost no one teaches you how to leave.

But there comes a moment when you know, when the grace you once carried for a situation has lifted. When prayer and trusted counsel have confirmed what your spirit already senses, when that inevitable moment arrives, understand this: the timing will never feel perfect. People who have benefited from your presence rarely celebrate your departure. Their resistance is not always malicious. It's often the direct result of the grief they're experiencing, as the thought of losing someone they may not have fully appreciated is now front and center.

> *(You might say, if they had valued your presence, they wouldn't have to feel your absence. But that's a book for another day.)*

I remember when I had to leave a position I had held for nearly ten years. I had poured myself into that place. I built deep relationships, achieved meaningful success, and established significant influence. But I knew the chapter was closing. Rather than rush out the door or be pushed through it, I spent over two years in discernment. When my release finally came, I left on my own terms, with the same grace I brought when I arrived. I gave two months' notice.

I offered to stay as long as needed to ensure a smooth transition. To this day, I carry an excellent relationship with that organization, and that, too, is part of the legacy of leaving well.

I will not pretend, however, that every departure goes smoothly. Sometimes, leaving gets messy. Sometimes people respond poorly, unfairly, or even harshly. In those moments, you do not have to descend to that level. Stay rooted. Stay grounded in your truth. Your growth will speak for itself. Your RESET will be its own testimony.

The depth of your healing is often correlated with how much you are willing to release.

✶ A Prayer ✶

Father, I come to You with open hands and an open heart. Show me what I am still holding that no longer serves my growth or my purpose. Give me the courage to release every weight, burden, and expectation that You never designed for me to carry. Fill the places I empty with Your peace, Your strength, and Your presence. Today, I choose release. In Jesus' name, Amen.

Key Takeaways

- Release is not failure. It is an alignment with who God is calling you to become.
- Not everything attached to you is assigned to you. Some burdens were never yours to carry.
- The three essential releases: the pressure to be everything, roles that no longer fit, and pain you keep replaying.
- God calls people to leave. Leaving can be a sign of obedience, not failure.
- The sacred exchange: what you release, God fills.

Chapter 5 — Reflection & Exercises

What are you still carrying that was never assigned to you?

What would you let go of if you truly believed you could survive without it?

Name one role, expectation, or relationship you have been holding onto past its season.

After releasing it, what do you want God to fill that space with?

____

____

____

____

Action Checkpoint

☐ I have identified what I need to release in this season.

☐ I have written honestly about what is holding me back.

☐ I have identified the one concrete step I'm willing to take this week.

RESET SESSION

What Will You Release?

Take time with each question below. Write honestly. Your first answer is usually the most truthful.

Name three things you are holding right now that are crushing you but were never truly assigned to you.

What role, obligation, or identity have you outgrown, but you're still holding because you're afraid of what releasing it means?

Write a brief 'letter of release' to something you've been carrying too long—an expectation, a person, a role, or a pain.

Release Declaration Checkboxes — I am releasing:

- ☐ The pressure to be everything to everyone.
- ☐ A role I have outgrown.
- ☐ The pain I keep replaying.
- ☐ The guilt I have been carrying that was never mine to hold.
- ☐ The fear of disappointing others by choosing my own healing.

Chapter 6

E: Embrace

Emotional Awareness

Emotions as God-Given Signals

Emotions are not the enemy. They are not signs of weak faith or insufficient spiritual maturity. Emotions are God-given signals of information about your internal world that, when honored, can guide you toward healing and alignment. When ignored, they migrate into your body, your behavior, and your relationships.

The Four Core Emotional Needs

Every human being has four core emotional needs: to be seen, to be safe, to feel significant, and to have a sense of belonging. Much of what we call emotional pain is, at its root, an unmet need in one or more of these areas. Much of the numbing, the performing, and the overextending you've been doing is an attempt to meet these needs in ways that were never designed to satisfy them.

Practicing Emotional Honesty

Emotional honesty is not emotional dumping. It is not venting without a filter or processing without boundaries. Emotional honesty is the intentional practice of naming what is true about your internal experience and bringing it, with appropriate vulnerability, to safe people and to God.

The Language of Emotions

Many people, particularly those raised in emotionally restrictive environments, struggle to name their emotions beyond "fine," "stressed," or "tired." Expanding your emotional vocabulary is not therapy talk. It is spiritual literacy. The Psalms model a rich and varied emotional language. David used words like abandoned, crushed, surrounded, safe, joyful, and afraid. We must be comfortable doing the same.

You cannot access what you will not acknowledge. Emotional honesty is the beginning of emotional freedom.

✶ A Prayer ✶

God, You created me with the capacity to feel, and You feel deeply too. Help me stop treating my emotions as problems to be managed and start receiving them as information You intended to guide me. Give me the courage to name what is true — to stop performing okay when I am not. Teach me the language of honest emotion. Help me bring my whole self to You, not just the parts I am proud of. In Jesus' name, Amen.

Key Takeaways

- ❖ Emotions are God-given signals, not signs of weak faith.
- ❖ The four core needs — to be seen, safe, significant, and to belong—drive much of human behavior.

- Emotional suppression doesn't eliminate pain. It relocates it.

- Emotional honesty is a spiritual practice, not a sign of instability.The Psalms permit us to bring our full emotional truth to God.

Chapter 6 — Reflection & Exercises

What emotion have you been most consistently pushing away in this season?

Which of the four core needs, seen, safe, significant, and belonging, feels most unmet right now?

What would it look like to practice emotional honesty with one safe person this week?

What emotions are you most afraid to feel? What do you think would happen if you let yourself feel them?

____

____

____

____

Action Checkpoint

- ☐ I have named one emotion I have been avoiding without judgment.
- ☐ I have identified one unmet core need and taken one step toward getting it met.
- ☐ I have practiced sitting with an uncomfortable feeling without trying to fix it.

RESET SESSION

Embracing Your Emotions

Take time with each question below. Write honestly. Your first answer is usually the most truthful.

What emotion have you been pushing away most persistently in this season? Name it. Describe what it feels like in your body.

____

____

____

____

If this emotion you've been avoiding could speak, what would it say to you? What does it mostly need you to know?

____

____

____

____

Embrace Checkboxes — I am choosing to:

☐ Name one emotion I have been avoiding without judgment.

☐ Identify one unmet core need and take one step toward getting it met.

☐ Practice sitting with an uncomfortable feeling for 5 minutes without trying to fix it.

☐ Talk to a safe person about one emotion I rarely share with anyone.

Chapter 7

S: Surrender

Trading Exhaustion for Trust

Stewardship vs. Control: The Critical Distinction

There is a critical difference between stewardship and control. Stewardship says: I am responsible for doing what I can with what God has entrusted to me, and I trust Him with the outcome. Control says: I must manage every variable, anticipate every threat, and ensure the outcome myself. The belief stems from the flawed idea that everything will fall apart if you don't.

Why We Hold On

Control is almost always rooted in fear. Fear of failure. Fear of disappointment. Fear of abandonment. Fear of what others will think. Fear that if you let go, God won't catch you. Fear that your faith isn't strong enough to survive the release.

Rest as Worship

In a culture that celebrates busyness and productivity, rest can feel like irresponsibility. For believers raised in traditions that equate busyness with faithfulness, Sabbath can feel like sin. But the Sabbath was not a suggestion. It was a commandment. A sacred rhythm built into the very structure of creation by a God who wanted you to practice trusting that the world would not fall apart in your absence.

The Jesus Model of Surrender

Jesus modeled surrender not as passivity but as the deepest act of trust. In Gethsemane, He said, "Not my will, but Yours." He was fully aware of the cost. He was not in denial. He was not performing spiritual strength. He was genuinely anguished. Out of that anguish, He chose surrender. Jesus was able to do this because He trusted the Father more than He feared the pain of the moment.

Surrender is not the absence of effort.
It is the presence of trust.

✶ A Prayer ✶

God, I confess that I have been trying to manage what only You can carry. I have been white-knuckling outcomes that were never mine to control. I am exhausted from the effort. Today, I choose to practice what I preach and release what I have been holding. Teach me the difference between faithful action and frantic control. I trust You with what I cannot see. In Jesus' name, Amen.

Key Takeaways

- Surrender is not giving up. It is trusting God with what you cannot control.
- The difference between stewardship and control is the difference between peace and exhaustion.
- Control is almost always rooted in fear. Fear-driven leadership eventually burns out.
- Rest is not irresponsibility. It is an act of worship and a practice of trust.
- Jesus modeled surrender as the highest form of faith. It's not a form of weakness, trust.

Chapter 7 — Reflection & Exercises

In what area of your life do you work the hardest to maintain control?

What are you afraid would happen if you surrendered this area to God?

What would a genuine Sabbath practice look like for you this week?

Where have you confused being responsible with being in control?

____

____

____

____

Action Checkpoint

- ☐ I have identified the area where my need for control is greatest.
- ☐ I have written an honest prayer of surrender for one specific area.
- ☐ I have scheduled at least one genuine rest period this week.

RESET SESSION

Practicing Surrender

Take time with each question below. Write honestly. Your first answer is usually the most truthful.

In what area of your life do you work the hardest to maintain control? What are you most afraid will happen if you let go?

____

____

____

____

How has your need to control cost you in your relationships, health, peace, or intimacy with God? Be specific.

____

____

____

____

Write a brief prayer of surrender for the specific area you most need to release. Let it be honest. Let it be real.

____

____

____

____

Surrender Checkboxes — I am surrendering:

☐ The outcome I have been trying to manage or control.

☐ My need to have all the answers before I take the next step.

☐ My fear of disappointing someone if I stop performing.

☐To rest as a spiritual practice this week.

Chapter 8

E: Engage

What Awakens Your Soul

Engagement as Spiritual Practice

After burnout strips you bare, one of the most important questions you can ask is: what actually gives me life? Not what I'm supposed to love. Not what makes me look productive, godly, or successful. What genuinely, authentically, consistently makes me come alive?

The Difference Between Obligation and Engagement

Obligation says yes because it fears disappointing someone. Engagement says yes because something in you is drawn toward it. Obligation depletes. Engagement replenishes. Obligation drains. Engagement fills. The reset life requires learning to distinguish between the two and having the courage to protect what gives you life.

Protecting What Gives You Life

One of the most spiritual things you will ever do is say no to the things that drain you so that you have something left for the things that matter. Protecting your energy is not selfishness. It is stewardship. You cannot pour from an empty cup. You cannot give what you do not have.

Re-engaging Your God-Given Design

You were not created to be productive. You were created to be purposeful. There is a meaningful difference. Productivity is about output. Purpose is about alignment. Burnout happens when you are producing constantly but living out of alignment with what God actually designed you to be.

Joy is not a reward for finishing your to-do list.
It is a signal pointing you toward your purpose.

✶ A Prayer ✶

God, show me what gives me life. Remind me who I was before I was shaped by the demands and expectations of others. I want to be fully alive, not just functional. Give me the courage to say no to what drains me and yes to what awakens me. Help me protect the practices and pursuits that keep me connected to You and to myself. In Jesus' name, Amen.

Key Takeaways

- ❖ Burnout disconnects you from the things that give you life. Re-engagement reconnects you.
- ❖ Obligation depletes. Engagement replenishes. Learning to tell the difference is essential.
- ❖ Protecting what gives you life is stewardship, not selfishness.

- ❖ You were created for purpose, not just productivity. Alignment beats output every time.
- ❖ Joy is a signal, not a luxury. Pay attention to what makes you come alive.

Chapter 8 — Reflection & Exercises

What activities or pursuits consistently make you feel most fully like yourself?

What childhood interests or passions did you abandon because they weren't practical or spiritual?

What would you do if you gave yourself one hour per week for something that gives you life?

What have you been saying yes to out of obligation that is stealing your capacity for engagement?

____

____

____

____

Action Checkpoint

- ☐ I have named three things that make me feel fully alive.
- ☐ I have scheduled at least one of them on my calendar this week.
- ☐ I have said no to one obligation that is robbing me of time for what gives me life.

RESET SESSION

Awakening Your Soul

Take time with each question below. Write honestly. Your first answer is usually the most truthful.

What did you love to do as a child, before you were shaped by obligation and expectation? List at least three things.

____

____

____

____

What activities or pursuits currently make you lose track of time? What makes you feel most fully like yourself?

____

____

____

____

What would it look like to protect one hour per week for something that gives you life? What would you have to say no to in order to say yes to this?

____

____

____

____

Engagement Plan Checkboxes — This month, I will:

☐ Name three things that make me feel fully alive.

☐ Schedule at least one of them on my calendar this week.

☐ Say no to one obligation that is robbing me of time for what gives me life.

☐ Share with one trusted person what I'm choosing to re-engage and why.

Chapter 9

T: Transform

Through Intentional Action

The Power of Rhythms over Resolutions

Transformation is not a moment. It is a movement. It is not a decision made once in a high-emotion moment. It is a series of small, intentional choices made consistently over time. Rhythms are the architecture of lasting change.

Three Rhythms for the Reset Life

Rhythm of Reflection: This is your daily practice of checking in with yourself. Not performing, not producing, simply being present to what is true inside of you. This might be journaling, silence, prayer, or a walk where you ask: What am I carrying? What do I need? What does God want to say to me today?

Rhythm of Renewal: This is the practice of intentionally replenishing what has been poured out. It might be physical rest, creative expression, meaningful relationship, time in nature, or whatever consistently refuels your particular soul.

Rhythm of Relationship: Transformation is not a solo endeavor. You need at least one person who knows your real story, who will tell you the truth, and who will hold you accountable to the person you are becoming.

The Non-Negotiable Nature of Rhythms

The question is not whether you have time for rhythms. The question is whether you can afford not to have them. The person without rhythms is the person who ends up back in burnout, wondering why nothing changed.

When You Fall Off the Rhythm

Life will interrupt. Seasons will change. You will have weeks where the rhythms get derailed. The reset life is not a perfect life. It is a life with a posture of return. Not shame. Return. Not self-condemnation. But return. When you find yourself experiencing situations that have knocked you off your feet, take the time to pause. Identify what is happening in that moment, name what it is, release the fear, frustration, anger, or anxiety that it's caused, then trust God to give you the specific wisdom and action steps that will get you back on course.

The reset life is not a perfect life. It is a life with a posture of return.

✶ A Prayer ✶

God, I want a transformed life. Not just a changed moment. Help me build the rhythms that will sustain what You are doing in me. Show me what reflection looks like for my particular soul. Show me what renewal requires in this season. Connect me to the right person for honest, grace-filled accountability. Make me patient with the process. I trust Your timing. In Jesus' name, Amen.

Key Takeaways

- ❖ Transformation is not a moment. It is a movement built on consistent rhythms.
- ❖ The three essential rhythms: reflection, renewal, and relationship.
- ❖ Without rhythms, even genuine breakthrough fades over time.
- ❖ When you fall off the rhythm, the posture is returned—not shame.
- ❖ Small, consistent actions over time produce more transformation than dramatic but unsustained resolutions.

Chapter 9 — Reflection & Exercises

What would a daily rhythm of reflection look like for you specifically, not theoretically?

____

____

____

____

What consistently renews you? Is it currently on your calendar?

____

____

____

____

Who is one person who could serve as an honest, grace-filled accountability partner?

____

____

____

____

What small, consistent action best represents the person you are becoming?

____

____

____

____

Action Checkpoint

☐ I have established one daily reflection practice.

☐ I have scheduled one renewal activity per week and protected it.

☐ I have identified one accountability partner and made the ask.

☐ I have chosen one small, consistent action that reflects who I am becoming.

RESET SESSION

Building Your Rhythms

Take time with each question below. Write honestly. Your first answer is usually the most truthful.

Rhythm of Reflection: What is one daily or weekly practice that will help you stay connected to your inner world?

____

____

____

____

Rhythm of Renewal: What specifically refuels you? What will you schedule into your week as a non-negotiable renewal practice?

____

____

____

____

Rhythm of Relationship: Who is one person you could invite into an accountable, honest relationship around your transformation?

____

____

____

____

Transformation Checkboxes — Starting this week, I will:

☐ Establish one daily reflection practice (journaling, prayer, meditation).

☐ Schedule one renewal activity per week and protect it.

☐ Identify one accountability partner and make the ask this week.

☐ Choose one small, consistent action that reflects who I am becoming.

☐ Review my progress at the end of this month and adjust as needed.

PART THREE

THE RESET LIFE

You have done the interior work. Now it is time to live it. These final chapters show what a reset life looks like in practice, not as a one-time event, but as a daily posture of alignment. You were not made to do this alone.

Chapter 10

The Reset Life

What Living from Alignment Looks Like

The reset life is not a destination you arrive at and remain forever unchanged. It is a daily choice. A continuous practice. A lifelong commitment to alignment over achievement. To be completely present, not caught up in busyness and activity. To be fully aligned instead of simply doing.

Alignment is not perfection. Aligned people still experience hard seasons, make mistakes, and face unexpected losses. But alignment changes how you navigate it all. When you are aligned, when your values, your choices, your energy, and your calling are pointing in the same direction, you have access to a quality of peace that is not dependent on circumstances.

Signs That You Are Living in Alignment

You make decisions from your values rather than your fears. You say no to the things that drain you without the crippling guilt. You feel genuinely excited about at least some of what you are doing. You can sit still without it feeling like negligence. Your relationships reflect mutuality and depth rather than performance and exhaustion. Your inner life and your outer life are telling the same story.

The Daily Practice of Reset

The reset life requires a daily practice. Not a daily performance. A practice says: I show up for this consistently, even when I don't feel like it, even when the results are invisible, and even when I fall short. The daily practice of reset is as simple as this: each morning, ask yourself one question before you begin your day. What am I carrying that is not mine to carry today?

Some days the answer is clear. Some days it takes a few minutes of quiet. But the practice of asking keeps you grounded and aware of your own interior world, rather than being swept along by everyone else's demands before you've even had a chance to move into your day.

Your Reset Ripples Outward

Here is what you may not have realized: your reset is not just about you. When you choose alignment over exhaustion, you model something that the people around you desperately need to see. When you draw a healthy boundary, you give the people in your life permission to do the same. When you ask for help, you normalize vulnerability for those who are watching. When you tell the truth about your struggle, you give someone else the courage to tell theirs.

Your healing creates space for someone else's healing. Your reset ripples outward.

✶ A Prayer ✶

God, thank You for reminding me that the reset life is not a destination but a daily returning to the life You intend for me to live. Help me to surrender anything that was never mine to carry.

Help me make decisions grounded in the purpose and values you have set for me. Forever remind me that you have not given me the spirit of fear but of love, power, and a sound mind. (II Timothy 1:7)

When the pressure to perform rises in my mind, quiet it. When the urge to prove myself to others returns, redirect it. Remind me that alignment with you is my primary goal, not personal achievement.

Let my inner and outer life tell the same story of your peace, love, and restoring power.

In Jesus Name.

Key Takeaways

- ❖ Alignment is a daily choice, not a destination you arrive at once.
- ❖ The daily practice of reset begins with one question: What am I carrying that is not mine to carry?
- ❖ Living in alignment does not mean the absence of difficulty — it means navigating difficulty from a stable center.
- ❖ Your reset is not just for you. It creates permission for everyone who is watching.
- ❖ The reset life prioritizes being over doing, alignment over achievement.

Chapter 10 — Reflection & Exercises

What does alignment feel like in your body? What does misalignment feel like?

What would a daily reset practice look like for you, specifically?

Where in your life have you been performing rather than actually living?

ho in your circle might benefit from watching you choose alignment over exhaustion?

____

____

____

____

Action Checkpoint

☐ I have designed my daily reset practice and written it down.

☐ I have identified at least one sign of alignment currently present in my life.

☐ I have committed to the daily practice for one week.

RESET SESSION

Living in Alignment

Take time with each question below. Write honestly. Your first answer is usually the most truthful.

Looking at the signs of alignment, which ones are present in your life today? Which ones are still developing?

___

___

___

___

Design your 'Daily Reset' practice. What is the one morning question or practice that will help you stay connected to your alignment each day?

___

___

___

___

What is the greatest threat to your alignment right now? Identify the pattern, person, or pressure most likely to pull you off center? What is your plan when that happens?

___

___

___

___

Alignment Checkboxes — My daily reset includes:

☐ A morning check-in question I ask myself every day.

☐ At least one boundary I am committed to holding this week.

☐ One intentional act of rest or renewal scheduled into my week.

☐ One relationship I am investing in that reflects my values.

☐ A monthly review of my alignment indicators.

Chapter 11

Resetting Together

Creating Communities of Restoration

Transformation in isolation is fragile. Humans were never designed to transform alone. From the earliest pages of Scripture, God declared that it is not good for us to be alone—not just romantically, but communally. We are wired for connection, for accountability, for the kind of honest relationship that holds us to who we are becoming, even when we forget.

What Accountability Is and Is Not

True accountability is mutual. It is filled with grace, not driven by shame. It's rooted in genuine love and a commitment to the other person's success and flourishing, not in the need to be right, to have power, or to manage someone else's behavior. It says, "I am for you." And because I am for you, I will share with you the truth in grace and love.

Accountability is not surveillance. It is not checking in to catch someone failing. It is not the person who texts you 47 questions every Monday morning to make sure you've hit your goals. It is the person who will sit with you when you've fallen short, who will not ask "did you do it?" but "how are you really?"

Solo transformation leaves you vulnerable. Partnered transformation often leads to sustainable results.

Finding the Right Person

Look for someone who is also committed to growth. Someone who can hold tension without immediately needing to fix you or it. Someone who will tell you the truth in love. (Truth without love is harsh, love without truth is enabling.) They must respect confidentiality and have the emotional and mental capacity for the relationship.

Resetting the Community: When the Church Chooses to R.E.S.E.T.

R.E.S.E.T. is not only for individuals. It is also a framework for communities of faith. When people are hurt by the church, the instinct is often to defend and protect the reputation. But if we are going to be the body of Christ, we must learn to respond to hurt differently.

Churches that are willing to reset must first recognize the harm. Recognition sounds like: "I am listening. I believe you experienced harm. I am sorry." Compassion must precede correction. Then they must examine the culture and extend the repair. Recognition without repair is incomplete. Apologies without structural change retraumatize.

✶ A Prayer ✶

God, You created me for community, not isolation. Lead me to the right person: someone committed to their own growth, someone safe with my struggles, someone who will tell me the truth in love, someone who will walk beside me. Give me the courage to reach out. Give me wisdom to choose well. Give me humility to be honest. In Jesus' name, Amen.

Key Takeaways

- Transformation in isolation is fragile. Humans were never designed to transform alone.
- True accountability is mutual, based in grace, and committed to honesty rather than performance.
- The church can use the R.E.S.E.T. framework too: recognize harm, examine culture, and extend repair.
- Confession to another human leads to healing. Shame dies in the light.
- You were never meant to reset alone. Find your person. Do this journey together.

Chapter 11 — Reflection & Exercises

Who in your life is currently your closest accountability partner? If you don't have one, who could you invite?

____

____

____

____

What has kept you from being fully honest with people who are close to you?

____

____

____

____

What would a reset-centered community look like for you? What would make it feel safe?

____

____

____

____

If you are in a church context, where do you see opportunities for your community to choose R.E.S.E.T.?

____

____

____

____

Action Checkpoint

☐ I have identified one person I trust with my real story.

☐ I have made a specific ask for accountability.

☐ I am showing up consistently—not just when I'm thriving, but when I'm struggling too.

RESET SESSION

Finding Your Person

Take time with each question below. Write honestly. Your first answer is usually the most truthful.

Who in your life right now feels safe enough to know the real story of what you've been going through? What makes them feel safe?

What would it look like for you to invite someone into an accountability relationship? What specifically would you share, and what would you ask of them?

What has kept you from being fully known in the community? What is the fear? What would change if that fear were no longer in charge?

Community Checkboxes — I am committing to:

☐ Identify one person I trust with my real story.

☐ Make a specific ask for accountability this week.

☐ Be honest with that person about where I am in my reset journey.

☐ Show up consistently. Not just when I'm thriving, but also when I'm struggling.

EPILOGUE

A LETTER TO THE FUTURE YOU

Dear Reader,

If you are reading this, you have completed a journey that most people are too afraid to begin. You have looked honestly at your exhaustion. You have permitted yourself to feel. You have released what no longer serves you. You have surrendered control. You have engaged what awakens you. You have taken intentional steps toward transformation.

But here is what I want you to know: this is not the end. This is the beginning.

The reset life is not a destination you arrive at and remain forever unchanged. It's a daily choice. A continuous practice. A lifelong commitment to alignment over achievement. To be completely present over busyness and activity. To be fully aligned instead of simply doing.

There will be days when you forget everything you've learned. When you overcommit and pour from an empty cup, and burnout calls out your name yet again.

On these days, come back to this framework. Not with shame for backsliding, but with grace for being human. R.E.S.E.T. again. As many times as you need. Because you are worth the ongoing work of staying aligned. You are worth the effort of protecting your peace. You are worth the courage it takes to keep choosing yourself.

The world needs what you have to offer. But it needs you whole. Not depleted. Healed, not hiding. Free, not performing. So keep resetting. Keep releasing. Keep embracing. Keep surrendering. Keep engaging. Keep transforming.

And know that every time you do, you are not only changing your own life. You are permitting someone else to change theirs.

Thanks for allowing me on this journey with you.

In appreciation,

Your reset is not complete. It is continuous.
And that is exactly as it should be.

K. L. Davenport

APPENDIX A

THE RESET WORKBOOK

The Complete Reset Assessment

Rate yourself in each area on a scale of 1 (depleted) to 10 (thriving). Be honest — this is your baseline.

Emotional Health

My ability to identify, feel, and process my emotions

Score (1-10): ___ *Note why you gave yourself this score:*

Spiritual Health

The quality of my relationship with God (not my religious performance)

Score (1-10): ___ *Note why you gave yourself this score:*

Physical Health

My rest, movement, nutrition, and body care

Score (1-10): ___ *Note why you gave yourself this score:*

Relational Health

The quality of my closest relationships

Score (1-10): ___ *Note why you gave yourself this score:*

Vocational Health

The alignment between my work and my purpose

Score (1-10): ___ *Note why you gave yourself this score:*

Mental Health

My ability to manage stress, anxiety, and negative thought patterns

Score (1-10): ___ Note why you gave yourself this score:

Boundaries

My ability to say no and protect what matters to me

Score (1-10): ___ Note why you gave yourself this score:

30-Day Reset Journal

Use the pages below to track your daily reset practice over the next 30 days. Each day, answer the three core questions.

Day 1

What am I carrying today that is not mine to carry?

____

____

____

What do I need from God today?

____

____

____

One intentional act of alignment I choose today:

____

____

____

Day 2

What am I carrying today that is not mine to carry?

What do I need from God today?

One intentional act of alignment I choose today:

Day 3

What am I carrying today that is not mine to carry?

What do I need from God today?

One intentional act of alignment I choose today:

Day 4

What am I carrying today that is not mine to carry?

What do I need from God today?

One intentional act of alignment I choose today:

Day 5

What am I carrying today that is not mine to carry?

____

____

____

What do I need from God today?

____

____

____

One intentional act of alignment I choose today:

____

____

____

Day 6

What am I carrying today that is not mine to carry?

____

____

____

What do I need from God today?

____

____

____

One intentional act of alignment I choose today:

____

____

____

Day 7

What am I carrying today that is not mine to carry?

What do I need from God today?

One intentional act of alignment I choose today:

Day 8

What am I carrying today that is not mine to carry?

What do I need from God today?

One intentional act of alignment I choose today:

Day 9

What am I carrying today that is not mine to carry?

What do I need from God today?

One intentional act of alignment I choose today:

Day 10

What am I carrying today that is not mine to carry?

What do I need from God today?

One intentional act of alignment I choose today:

Day 11

What am I carrying today that is not mine to carry?

____

____

____

What do I need from God today?

____

____

____

One intentional act of alignment I choose today:

____

____

____

Day 12

What am I carrying today that is not mine to carry?

____

____

____

What do I need from God today?

____

____

____

One intentional act of alignment I choose today:

____

____

____

Day 13

What am I carrying today that is not mine to carry?,

____

____

____

What do I need from God today?

____

____

____

One intentional act of alignment I choose today:

____

____

____

Day 14

What am I carrying today that is not mine to carry?

____

____

____

What do I need from God today?

____

____

One intentional act of alignment I choose today:

____

____

Day 15

What am I carrying today that is not mine to carry?

____

____

____

APPENDIX B

FOR MINISTRY LEADERS AND MINISTRY WORKERS

Ministry leadership carries a unique burden. You are expected to have the answers while silently carrying your own unprocessed pain. You are expected to pour out while rarely being poured into. You are expected to model faith while privately wrestling with doubt. And because you are the shepherd, there is often no one watching out for you.

This appendix is for you specifically. The R.E.S.E.T. framework applies to you not as a leader who deploys it for others, but as a human being who needs it for yourself first.

Signs That a Ministry Leader Needs a Reset

You dread going to the church you once loved. Your sermons feel hollow even when the congregation responds. You minister to others' grief while your own goes unattended. You have stopped praying except in public. You have confused busyness with calling. You are more afraid of disappointing people than of misrepresenting God.

The Permission You May Be Waiting For

You have permission to be human. You have permission to not have all the answers. You have permission to see a counselor and not call it a crisis. You have permission to take a sabbatical. You have permission to tell your congregation: "I am in a season of reset, and I am choosing wholeness over performance."

The most powerful sermon you may ever preach is the one in which you are honest about your own need for a reset. Because the people in your congregation are watching to see if what you preach is something you actually live.

R.E.S.E.T. for Ministry Leaders

Release the version of ministry that has become about your ego, your sense of importance, or what you can gain or have access to.

Embrace the emotions you have been suppressing beneath the weight of spiritual leadership.

Surrender the illusion that the church, ministry, or program cannot function without you. Remember, it is God's church.

Engage the calling you were originally set apart for, not the machine, role, or set of responsibilities it has become.

Transform your culture by modeling the kind of rest, grace, appreciation, and compassion you would like your team to display.

APPENDIX C

RESET FOR ORGANIZATIONS

Organizations burn out just as individuals do. The symptoms look different — high turnover, disengagement, mission drift, toxic culture — but the root causes are often the same: survival mode as a permanent operating system, suppressed conflict, and the absence of psychological safety.

The R.E.S.E.T. framework scales from individual to organizational:

Release

What policies, structures, or cultural expectations are no longer serving the mission? What roles have people been assigned that drain them and misuse their gifts? What assumptions from an earlier season are being carried into a new one where they no longer apply?

Embrace

Does your organization have psychological safety — the ability for people to name what is true without fear of retaliation? Is conflict addressed honestly or suppressed? Are employees and volunteers encouraged to bring their whole selves, or only the productive parts?

Surrender

What outcomes are leadership white-knuckling rather than stewarding? Where is fear of failure driving control rather than trust driving empowerment?

Engage

Are people in roles that align with their gifts? Is there genuine joy in the work, or only survival? What practices renew the team's collective spirit?

Transform

What measurable commitments will the organization make to transform and sustain internal organizational change? Who is accountable for implementation? What structures ensure the reset becomes a rhythm and not a one-time retreat?

ABOUT THE AUTHOR

Rev. K. L. Davenport, M.T.S. is a minister, coach, and organizational consultant with over two decades of experience assisting individuals, leaders, and faith communities through burnout, spiritual transition, and personal transformation.

Drawing from both theological training and evidence-based coaching methodologies, Rev. Davenport's work offers a Christian guide for individuals seeking to integrate, align, and transform their lives after burnout and significant life transitions.

As the creator of the R.E.S.E.T. framework, Rev. Davenport has guided organizations and individuals through the process of releasing what no longer serves them, embracing emotional honesty, surrendering control, re-engaging their God-given individual and organizational gifts, while transforming through intentional action.

Rev. Davenport holds a Master of Theological Studies (M.T.S.) from Vanderbilt University and a Bachelor's Degree in Political Science from Fisk University. He has served in pastoral leadership roles, worked on numerous civic and community engagement initiatives at the local, state and national level, as well as provided coaching and consulting that have generated sustainable results in both individuals and organizations. His firsthand experience of burnout, grief, and the process of realignment informs every page of this book.

R.E.S.E.T. When The Strong One Breaks is Rev. Davenport's debut book. It serves as a testimony to what God can do when we finally choose honesty over performance and alignment over achievement.◆◆◆

Made in the USA
Coppell, TX
22 June 2026

83163243R00075